Stretching Silver Through Blue Haze

Stretching Silver Through Blue Haze

poems by

Lawrence Gregory

photographs by

Birgit Gutsche

Shanti Arts Publishing
Brunswick, Maine

Stretching Silver Through Blue Haze

Published by Shanti Arts Publishing
Interior and cover design by Shanti Arts Designs

Shanti Arts LLC
193 Hillside Road
Brunswick, Maine 04011
shantiarts.com

Printed in the United States of America

ISBN: 978-1-941830-66-6 (softcover)
ISBN: 978-1-941830-67-3 (digital)

Library of Congress Control Number: 2017939169

Acknowledgements

Grateful acknowledgment is made to the editors of the following publications in which these poems have appeared:

"Canyon" in *Mountain Gazette*

"The Loneliest Road" in *Red Rock Review*

"Where Barns Once Stood" in *Yampa Valley Voice*

"Fifteen Below Zero" and "On This November Day" in *Malpaís*

"Monument" in *Crosswinds Poetry Journal*

"In This Moment" in *Santa Fe Literary Review*

I am a part of all that I have met;
Yet all experience is an arch wherethro'
Gleams that untravelled world, whose margin fades
For ever and for ever when I move.

— *Ulysses*
Alfred, Lord Tennyson

Contents

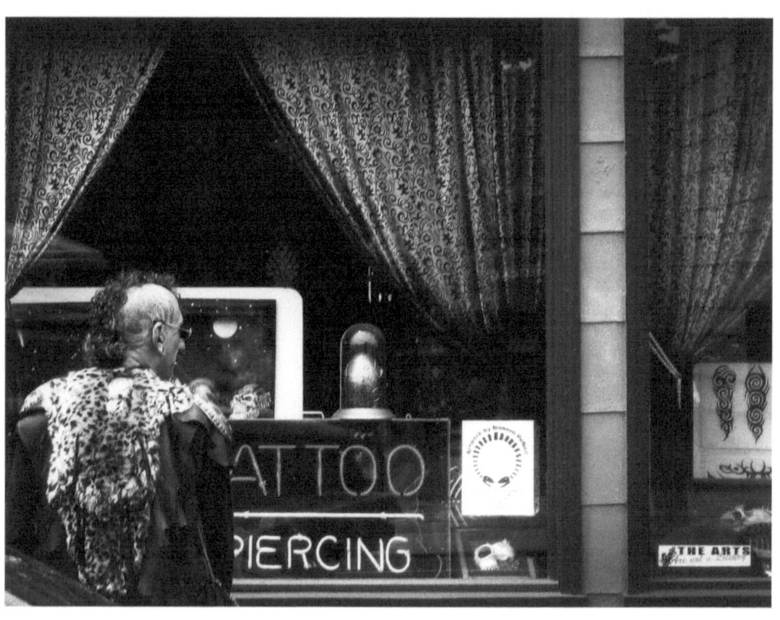
ATTOO
PIERCING
THE ARTS

Acceptance

We are never quite ready
for what comes next.

Even the inevitable

when it arrives
dressed to kill

wearing its hard
spangled certainty on its sleeve

surprises.

Canyon

Would that I could be content
to sit with you on the bank
beneath the warm sun
and watch the green water,
streaked by the ages,
weave through this canyon of stone
toward the sea.
But I will strip naked
and sink into the flow,
as if to embrace the startling chill
would quell this longing in my bones.

In This Moment

In this moment it is enough
for the two of us to sit here in the sage and
feel the chill press of wind against our backs.

No need for me to conjure words and
send them scudding through the stillness like
those clouds flaring red in the western sky.

In this moment it is enough
for you to wrap your arms around your knees,
draw them tight against your chest, and shiver a bit.

There is time enough
before we reach the borderlands
and in the crossing say goodbye.

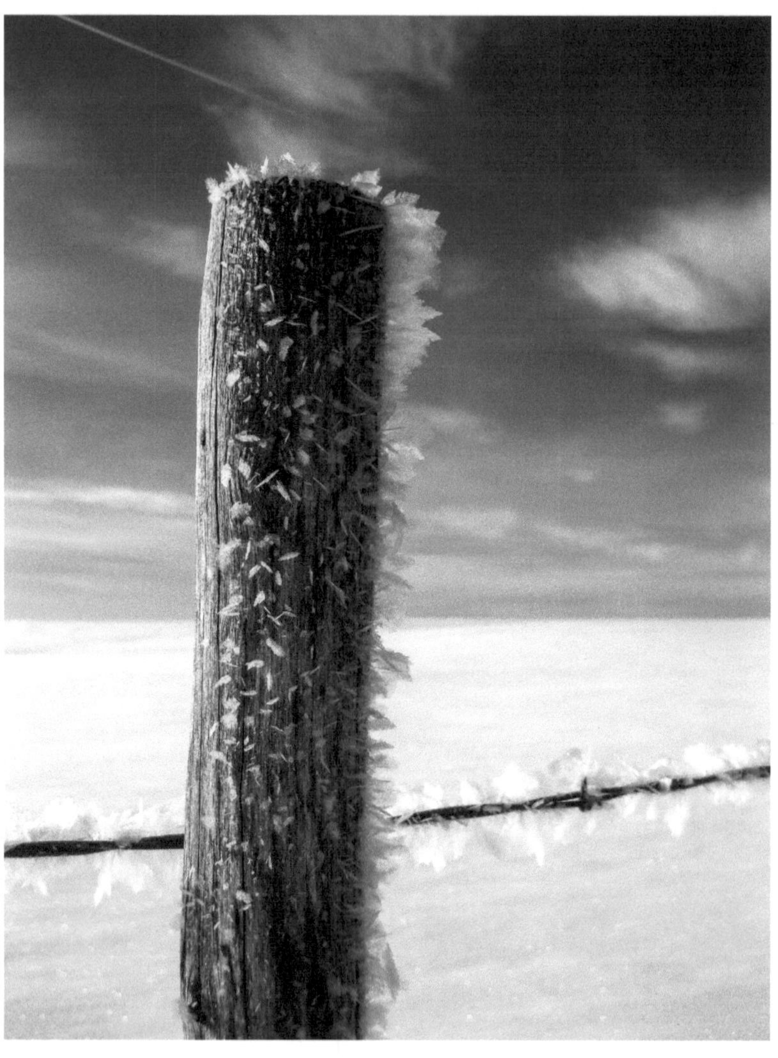

Fifteen Below Zero . . .

and yet grateful
to want for nothing more
than the quiet cold;

the brilliant sunlight
pouring through the windows
of this silent house.

Beyond the frosted panes
all the world's a panic —
frantically running from

or fighting for
the most outlandish
superstitions.

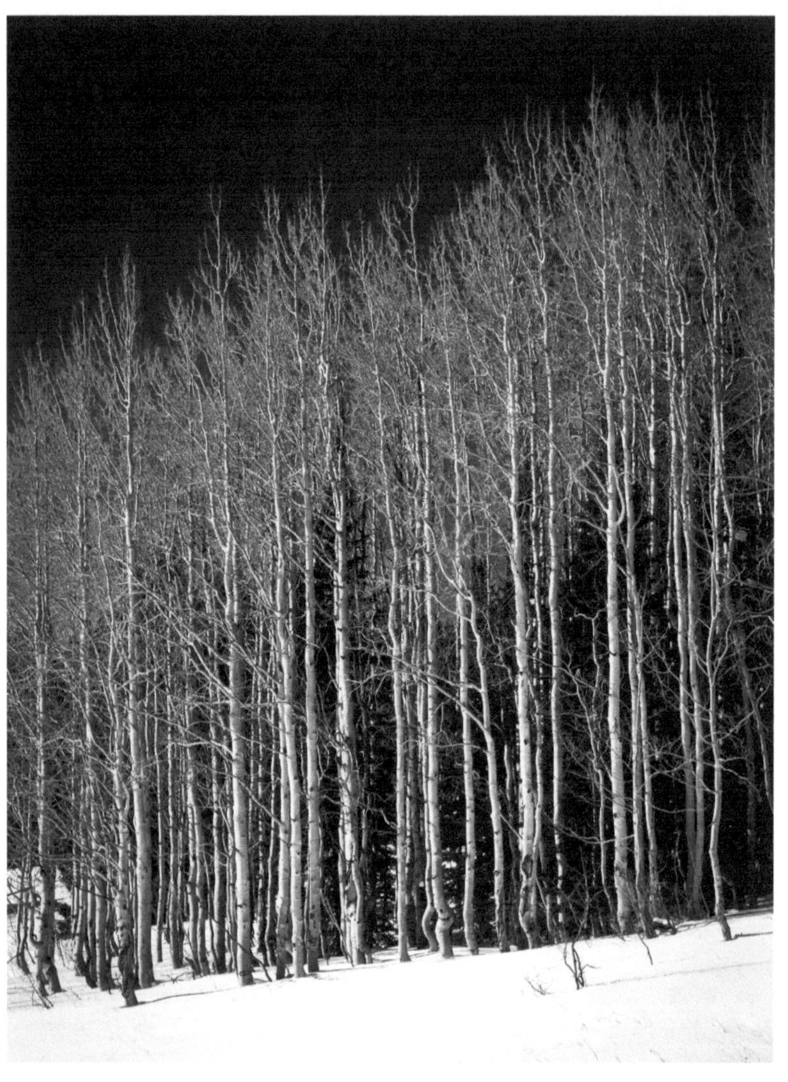

On This November Day

Today I did not earn a single cent.
I did not ride a bicycle or run
or swim or lift iron weights in the gym.

I did not drive to town for groceries
or download music from the internet.
I paid no homage to the GDP.

I did not purchase stocks or bonds nor try
to hedge life's bets against catastrophe.
I had the chance but did not sell my soul.

Instead, I sat in the November sun
and with a freshly sharpened pencil sketched
a picture of a solitary tree

leaning into the angled autumn light.
A twisted tree, stalwart against the wind.
A leafless aspen silent like the rest

but standing out from the glade of ordered
ranks guarding the line of separation
between home and the doings of the world.

I drew the tree as best I could although
noticing was all that really mattered.

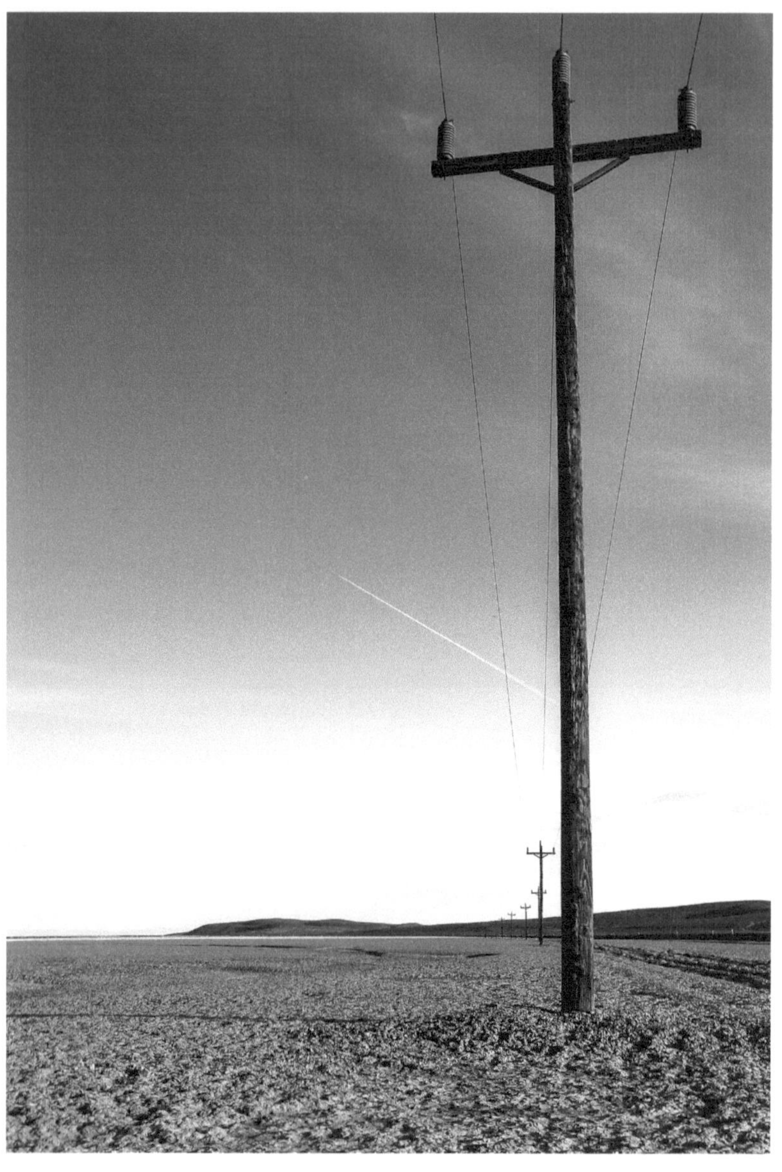

The Loneliest Road

In Fallon there are fighter jets and cows
and country music, God, and baseball caps
perched high on furrowed brows and memories
and women with big hair and bigger hearts
for men who work the land in faded blues.

From there the journey starts for those with time.
A lonely road best traveled without plans
in morning sun without intention's glare
on asphalt stretching silver through blue haze
and sagebrush tang and birdsong on the breeze.

Old love affairs are traced beside the road
in uppercase with rocks from ancient days
and we are left to wonder what remains.

The desert mice leave scrimshaw in the sand
as cirrus clouds and contrails stain a sky
so otherworldly blue it holds us fast
in reverential thought — or is it fear
of emptiness; the vast expanse of life?

And still the highway bends through solitude
to distant ranges far beyond this stage
where shadow dancers skim the folded dunes
while we abide together silently
content to share the loneliness and light.

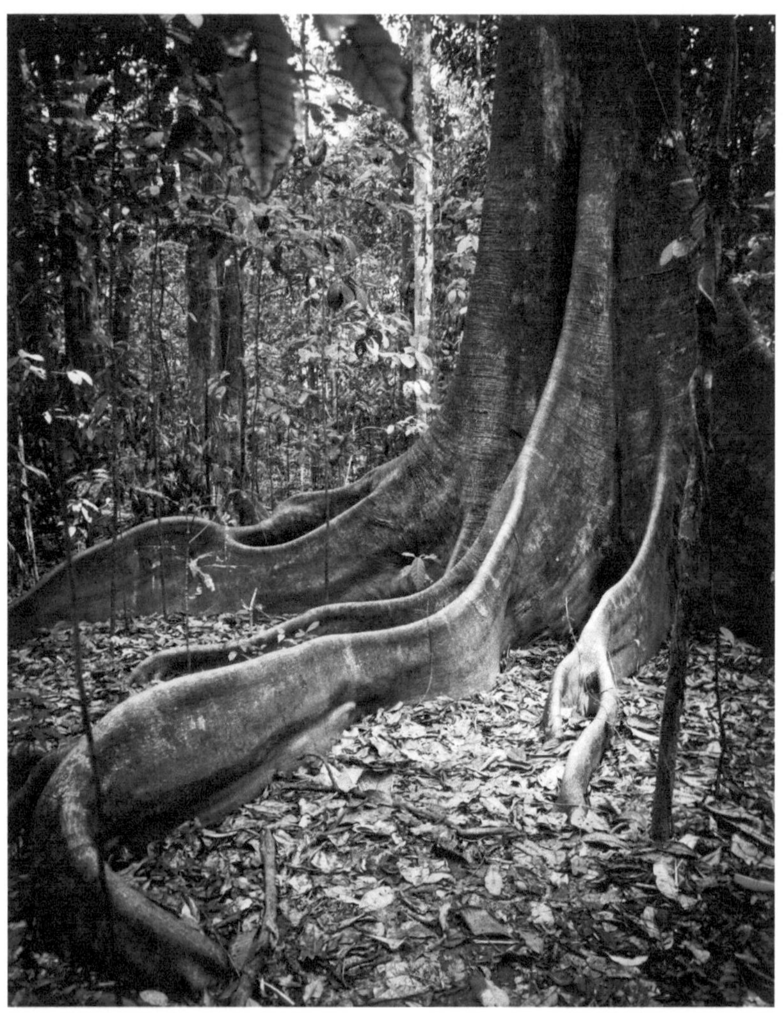

While We Lie Resting . . .

in this erotic air
still dripping from the storm

butterflies beat their gaudy wings
in the fragrant eddies

blood-red birds knife their way
through a slow green heat

where more things lurk unseen
than will ever be revealed.

In these jungle latitudes
hangs a sensual malaise

through which a spent leaf
spirals to the forest floor

where it waits to become
leaf again or vine

or maybe snake.
Jaguar is a possibility —

it makes no difference to the leaf.
So it simply rests

in the slow green heat.

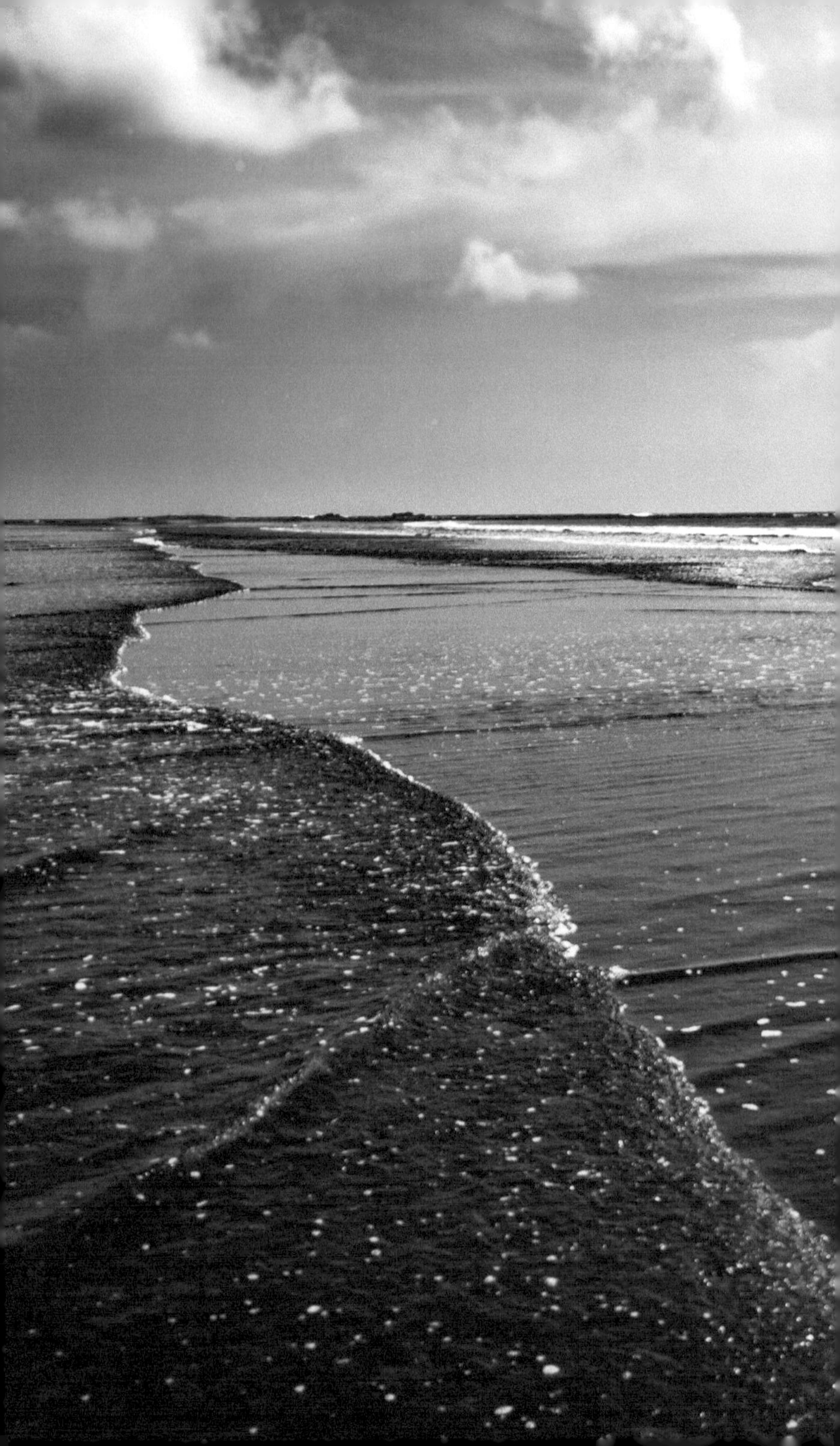

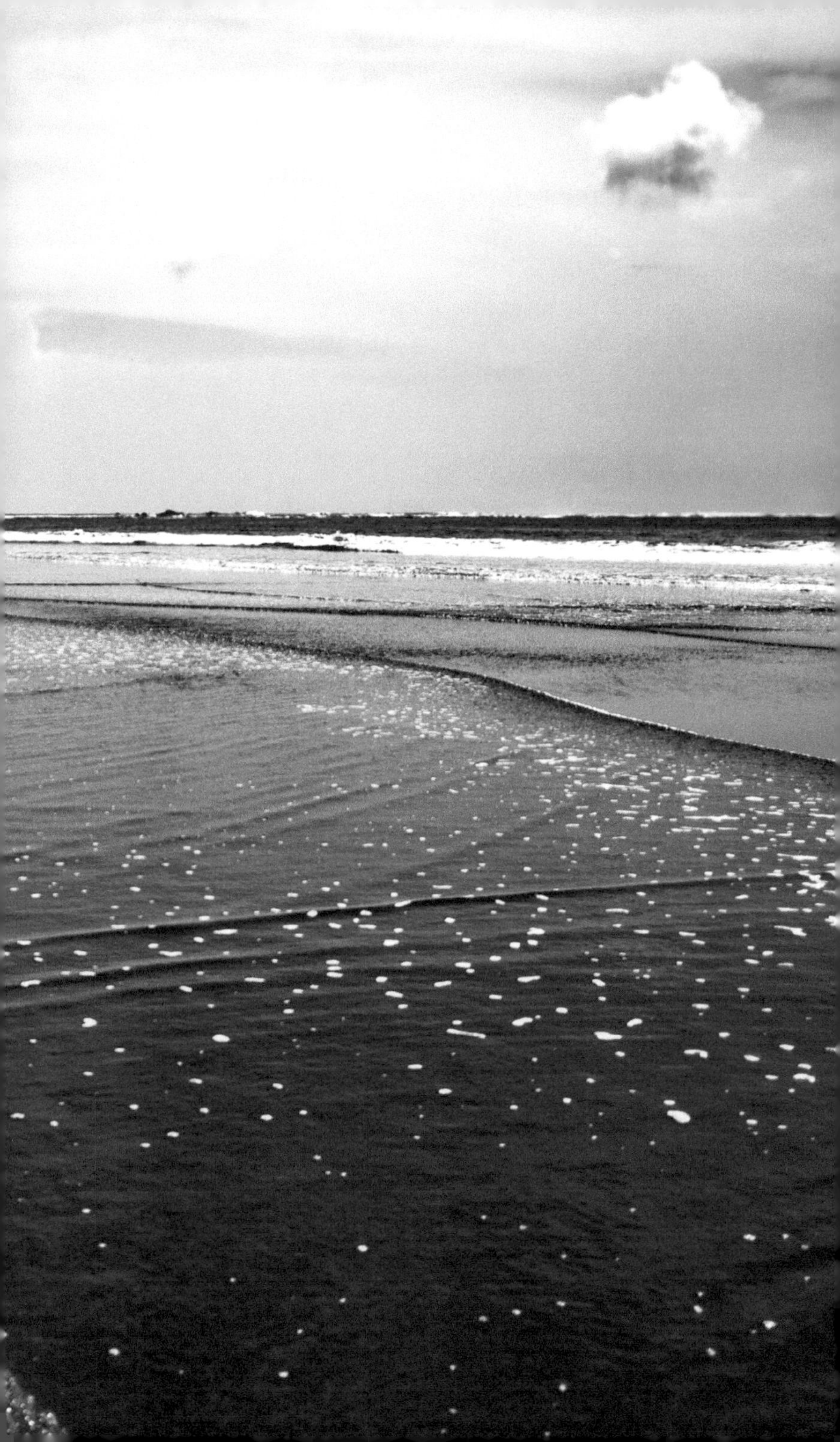

Liberation

How sweet to rest here on this empty shore
and watch the sun undress the beach once more.

With nothing left and no place I can hide
there are no options but to watch this tide

recede into the distance where the night
begins to yield its darkness to the light.

I'll walk across the liberated sand
into the morning sea where I can stand

and let the broken waves wash over me.
Alone once more but grateful to be free.

On the Road To Love

Although we've traveled far along the spine
Of continents in search of solitude,
We'll never know a silence more profound
Than what we knew before we left our home.

These mountains are just mountains in the end
They rise and fall and crumble into dust
And like their glaciers melting in the sun,
The past gives back whatever ground it gained

And leaves a shattered wasteland at our feet.
So come my dear, no need to linger here
Among these stones that punctuate the ground
Of yesterday — it's time to journey on.

And even if I never learn to love,
It's good to know you think I can and should.

Monument

I slept in this place first with you, although
I'd wandered past so many times before
When I was young. Who knew so long ago
We'd be together sleeping here and more?

On this desert rim rock, a better floor
You could not find, and no finer ceiling
Than these radiant stars, their ancient store
Of incandescent light a revel streaming

Through this solstice night, this pulsing naked
Night. Oh, love! Dream with me beneath this sky
'Til the star-set brings the rise of sacred
Revelation. Oh, love! Can you and I

Let go this nervous tendency to roam
And strive instead to make this land our home?

On This Afternoon

On this afternoon
of enchanted light

and Piñon smoke
curling toward sunset

you can take photographs
and I can write poetry

then together we'll walk
beside the clear river

knowing nothing else matters
beyond our languid drifting

toward evening's recline

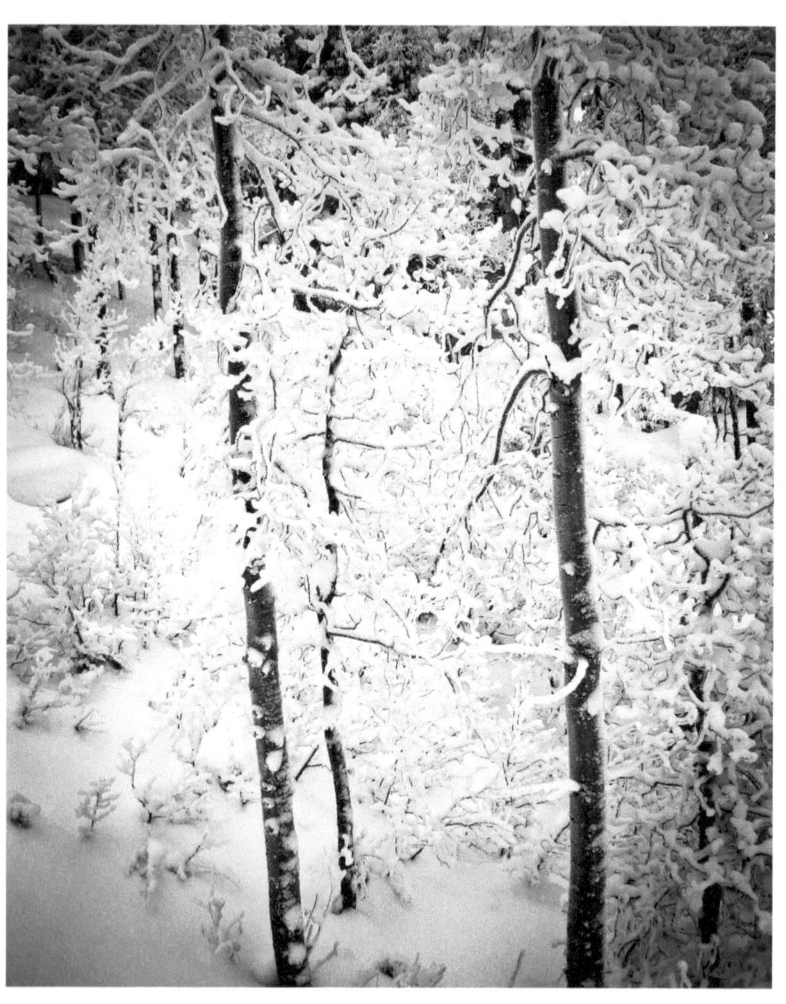

Snowfall

I want you to stay.

Rest with me in the silence
before this day

like every day

unravels in the onslaught and clamor
beyond our woods.

The snow is falling.
Listen . . .

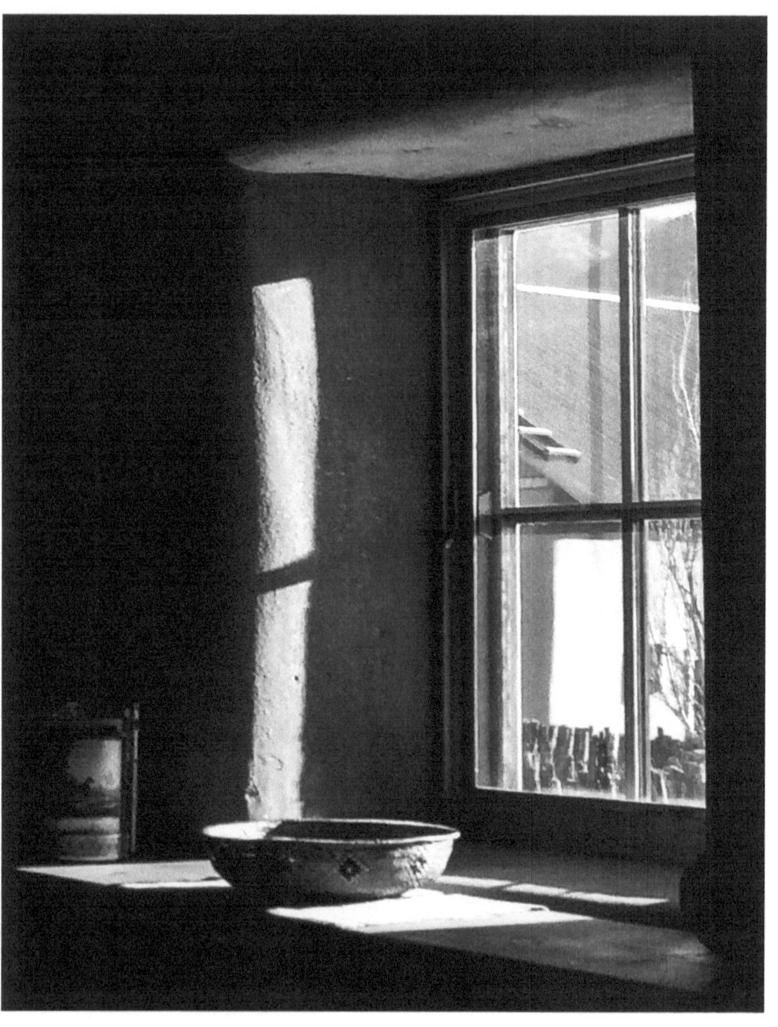

Recollection

Despite the sunlight's urgent beckoning
after so much April disappointment

we stayed in reading Pablo Neruda,
drinking lusty red wines from Argentina —

Cabernet and Malbec nurtured on the
flanks of the Andes' precipitous rise.

And your hips rose on that late afternoon
crest of surrender's easy ecstasy.

Weeks later, abandoned to solitude,
I search for traces of your existence.

Only the memory of your musky
scent still clings to the faded cotton sheets.

But in this blast of vernal loneliness
I cannot bear the thought of slipping in

between the layers of recollection
alone and longing for the disappeared.

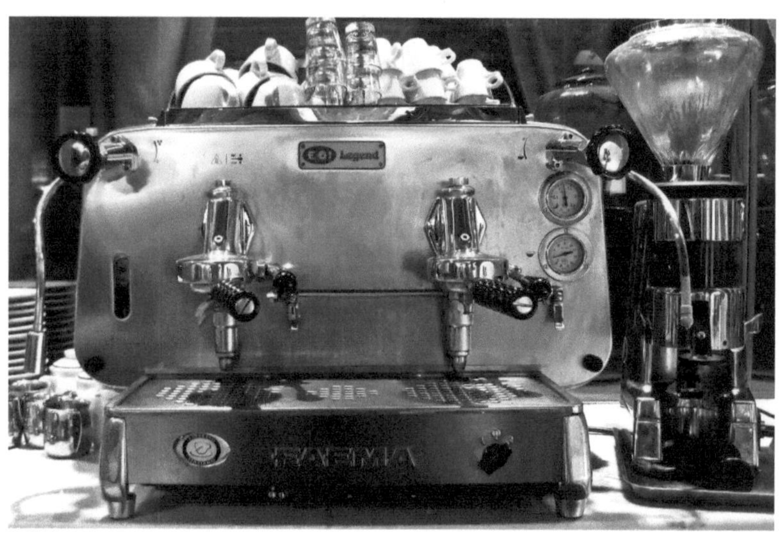
Legend
FAEMA

Is Yesterday a Better Thing Unknown?

It doesn't happen often but today
I calmed the anxious voices in my head
And chose to linger for awhile in bed
Let you be first to rise and glide away.

I felt your hand slide gently from my hip
And sensed a hesitation to retreat
From last night's love still tangled in the sheets.
You brushed a phantom kiss across my lip

And left me here to mingle with a dream—
A yesterday long past but still in flood.
Old love affairs still coursing through my blood
Mean nothing now to me but yet they seem

To energize the passion that we share.
Sometimes I'd like to learn a thing or two
Of love affairs you've had, the men you knew
But often think it better not to care.

Is yesterday a better thing unknown?
Should we conceal old lovers in the crowd
Clothe history in secrecy's dark shroud?
I'd ask right now, but best you're on your own

To share espresso with your memory
Of Italy—the burnished lovers left
Breathless and spent, so hopelessly bereft
In alabaster villas by the sea.

Reconstruction

Most days
I find a way
to break her heart.

Luckily
she finds a way
to cobble it back together

so that it still beats
still yearns
and beyond all reason

still loves me.

Stranded

Our breath no longer mingling I am left
alone in your bed adrift in emptiness.
I sense the heaving steel-gray ocean depth
and worry once more of being stranded
without you here on this desolate shore.

I watch the tide — incessant surging swell —
lapping at a thin line of lonely beach
littered with driftwood, pebbled with cold stones
sea-polished smooth and slick, and the dark sand
salted with shattered seashells white in death.

I hear the unsettled seabirds shrieking,
circling far above the restless sea,
while in the mist and uncertain winter
light the distant western islands vanish.

Wandering through your empty house, hurling
curses at the relentless Northwest rain,
I sip from a steaming mug of coffee
and consider washing last night's dishes,
or suicide, here among the brooding
western cedar and old growth Douglas fir.

Maybe It's Because I Read Hemingway Today

I cannot sleep, although I am tired,
because it is hot and the wind is loud
in the tall trees and I have been thinking
about your unadorned beauty.

Maybe it's because I read Hemingway
today that I've been comparing your elegance
to his bare-naked prose.

There is little difference between the way
his sentences stride across the page —
such long-legged athleticism and grace! —
and the way you arrived at the gallery last night.

It was the opening for a promising young artist
and the room was teeming with chic literati
and you were wearing a simple black dress
and I could see how, even at fifty,
you still turn the heads of men half your age.

Fly

A father must against his will let go
and grant his daughter freedom and bestow
a priceless gift transcending trifles bought—
a sacred life of independent thought.

To you my girl I offer this dear gift;
I'll cast my expectations far adrift.
So live the dreams you've fashioned in your heart
is my advice to you—I'll have no part

of chanting exhortations in your ears.
Embrace the life you've worked toward all these years
and fly my sweet into that brilliant sky
beyond the clouds of doubt and know that I

will celebrate with you your rising star.
You're on your own but I am never far.

Without Some Kind of Anchoring Punctuation

Despite the urgent red flag warnings
it's no surprise to find

yours is the only empty slip
within this safe harbor.

I know you're out there
far beyond the sheltering reef

writing your endless story
across the open water

in a spiraling hurricane of run-on
oceanic sentences

churning the placid blue deep into theatre
writ large in sea foam and salt spray.

Without some kind of anchoring punctuation
there's nothing to stop your constant running

with the wind — unfathomable the convoluted
consequences left in your wake!

Perhaps a comma would be useful —
a slackening wind —

some way to catch your breath without
coming to a full stop —

that would be disastrous.

Not for the likes of you to risk
floundering,

or end up like
a derelict Spanish galleon

long ago run aground
on an uncharted Caribbean shoal,

her slack sails still
searching for a breeze;

the sun-bleached crew of skeletons
still harboring their dreams.

Eighty Two

Because just before the rain finally quit
the room no longer seemed to fit the two
of us, I went down to the shore to watch
the nervous sea still churning from the storm.
Never mind the wind still bending the palms
and the incessant ringing in my ears
which wasn't really a ringing — not like
church bells, not like the rustic bells jangling
from the story book herd of goats I watched
trundling down Zermatt's *Bahnhofstrasse*
every morning and every afternoon
while waiting for the ice to melt above
the *Hörnlihütte*. Not like bells at all.
It was more a whistling, a constant rush
of wind trafficking through my head like the
roar of the freeway cleaving the rolling
hills below my mother's house in Marin, or
like the roar of the crowd coming from the
transistor radio hidden beneath
my pillow summer nights when the Dodgers

were playing. I'd sometimes drift off to sleep
listening to Vin Scully's play-by-play
while down the hall the two of them went on
drinking and arguing about whatever
it was they always argued about — his
chronic philandering mostly. Which begs
a question or two if one was inclined
to go there, which I'm not because, really,
it's hard enough standing here on this beach
thinking of them and remembering those days
and all their nights spent entertaining guests —
he sporting the latest 60s fashion,
she wrapped in a classic evening gown, her
bare arms sheathed in black satin cocktail gloves —
hard enough suddenly realizing
it's her eighty second birthday today
and that even if I could I wouldn't
send flowers or call because over the
years I've tried to understand, even tried
forgiveness once, but that glove didn't fit.

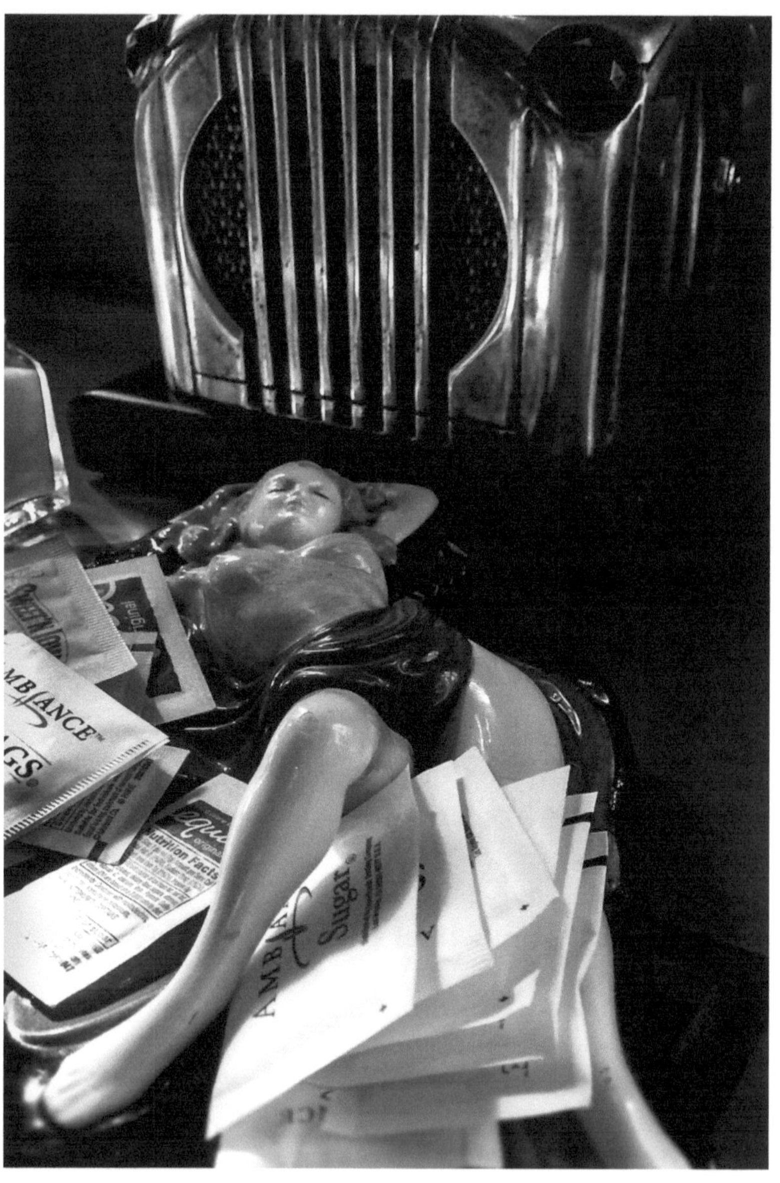
Nutrition Facts
Sugar

Thrilling

My father's was a frequent face at all the L.A. parties.
He gladly joined the multitude of guests

tripping and sharing each other
like monkeys — it was the 60s after all.

Trust me, he said, *it was thrilling.*
And despite what others say,

he left no erotic regrets clinging to the spent casing
shining on the bloody floor.

So you can't blame me for entertaining
dangerous urges.

Call it a twisted tradition if you like,
but in my day we had to blow off steam —

it wasn't an easy gig advising long
then selling short when you knew the score.

What's more, there were all the nubile
daughters of tycoons to contend with,

their firmly nippled breasts craved satisfaction
and bloodstained diamonds. Don't get me wrong,

I gladly paid their price — after all
it was an easy currency to come by.

And if I get the chance, I'll gladly
pay to taste ambition's sex once more.

What for?
Trust me, it's thrilling.

Extraordinary

Mother kept voracious tigers
and finches caged in the orchard

she said the sweetest fruit
hangs highest in the tree

but even in high heeled shoes
her ladder wasn't tall enough

so she buckled up and headed
out into the desert waste

her reflection rippling
across the altered sunrise

of our extraordinary exile

Father was a rock
and a spy

he wore a raincoat summer
and winter

doing his lonely work
in the vaults of bleeding banks

crouched in windswept cemeteries
kneeling at abandoned altars

even tightrope walking in the circus
when it landed in our town

which was always

❖

Sister was no ordinary schoolgirl
despite all the usual indications

not like the other flittering
hopscotch children

two-stepping toward
tomorrow

she kept her butterfly wings
rolled tight against her back

preferring the intrigue and
musty shelter of mushrooms

to any tree house

They say I've become
an extraordinary artist

but sinking my teeth
into desire blood and death

is just one way
to entertain boredom

there's also the journey
this descent out of wellness

which feels pretty damn good
at the moment

like a morning smoke
and the Sunday *Times*.

Grandmother In the Clouds (In Memoriam)

I've been sitting for hours on an old
wrought iron chair thinking of you because
when I was a boy we used to sit on

similar chairs under a bright summer sky
eating ice cream and watching the clouds,
which is what I've been doing this morning.

Not eating ice cream, but sitting outside
in the warm morning sun observing the
shredded remnants of last night's thunderstorm

shape shift up the flanks of sacred Taos Mountain,
a place you said you'd like to visit again
knowing all the while you weren't long for this

world. Something about the enchanting light
you wanted to experience once more
before finally fading into black—

the way it illuminates the landscape
and soul. *It would be glorious*, you said,
to live in such dazzling clarity.

Terrifying too, the revelation.
Which is perhaps the reason I've come to
be here now at the foot of this mountain

watching the clouds hover and heave in the
crystalline light; noticing their rhythm.
it's a kind of ethereal breathing

the way the gossamer veils undulate
in the rarefied atmosphere, riding
the warming currents higher and higher

to the glistening snow-dusted summit
where they hesitate a moment before
letting go into the blue oblivion.

Such grandeur and grace on the path to their
inevitable annihilation.

It's Difficult to Say . . .

but you
should have

(could have)

refused the dessert
passed on the nightcap

no doubt
would have

had you known
what was to come.

You could have
walked away in that red dress

(should have).

What is your address?
Have you read my poems?

The Haikuist

Caught out in the rain
She counts the wet syllables
Dripping on her page

Recess

I watch the children
on this green field
run between white lines.

They're still elbows, ankles,
knees and laughter
seems time enough

but then too soon
they'll be sought after.
Oh let them run!

I hear the cogs
the grinding gears
see the coming soldier years.

Oh let them run
outside the lines
unfettered by the rules!

Am I the teacher or the fool?
I hear the school bell chime
the end of recess

now it's time
to march them back to class —
the ordered desks

the lesson plans
the molding into
citizens.

Oh let them run
while there's still light
I hear the footfalls of the night.

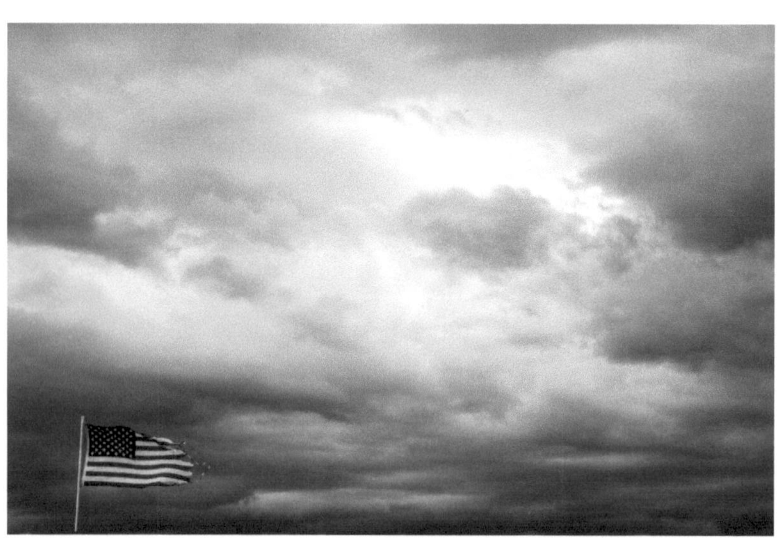

Homeland Insecure

Waving Old Glory
Ensconced in top secret courts
Tyranny listens

The Patriot Act
Wrapped in the Red White and Blue
Is anything but

I'm fear come calling
Verizon capitulates
Can you hear me now?

City of Angels

City of Angels
Land of Dreamers
matinée idols and
literary rascals

we were all once
actors and dancers
on that stage
but now turn the page

a stutter step
stiletto strut
ballet to the music
of a razor-wired sad song

hands up
don't shoot
I can't breathe
black lives never mattered

city under siege
with all its battered refugees
arcing through the night
too tight to notice

apparitions.

City of Angels
Land of demons
long thought dead
they're still dancing in my head

Please mother can you spare
the time
or bust another rhyme
or reason for these crimes

against our sanity?

Here comes another
dash cam brother
the latest actor on the stage
of neighborhood outrage

A Technicolor rampage
coming to your town.
The revolution is being televised
streaming live

across this drive-thru nation
of justice fornication
and private prison subjugation
Is that your God of salvation?

There's no mercy I can see.
Is that you?
Is that me?
Is that all of we?

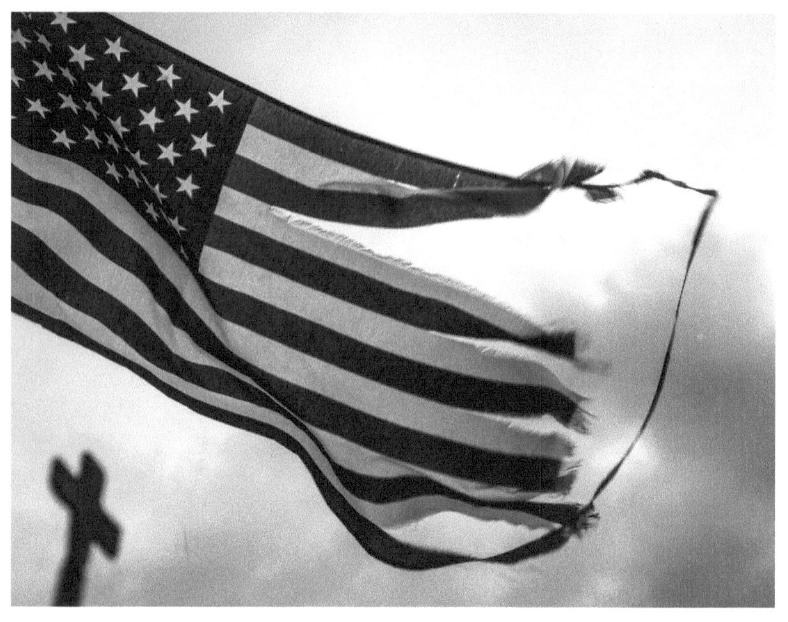

May 2, 2011

Have we achieved a noble end?
Does murder serve to make amends
for all our sorrow; will revenge

exacted on a terrorist
exalt the holy Eucharist;
bring back our loved ones from the mist?

They rest in peace so why do we
insist upon hostility;
invoke a false morality?

Ordained by those who live in fear,
the soldiers with their killing gear
strike out in anger every year

proclaiming violence will redeem
the sins of nations and the stream
of others who as in a dream

insist on living in the past.
As long as rage and hatred last
we'll never stop the hopeless cast

of characters whose ranks will swell;
they'll praise the day the towers fell
while we in pain will always dwell.

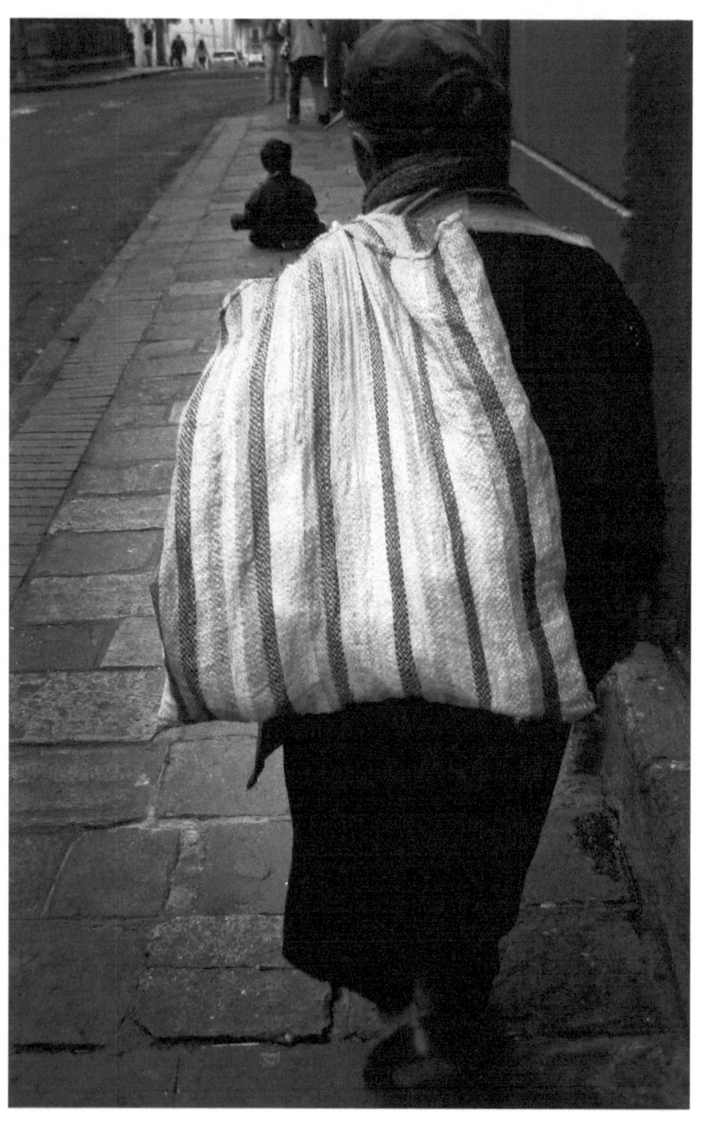

Ecuador After the Conquest (Para ti, mi hermano)

You and I sit in the shade drinking
imported red wine, savoring mangoes
eating thinly sliced beef from Argentina
and watch innocence squandered
for a shine on a shoe.

Urchins teem the cobbled streets, hobbled
men haul history's twisted limbs against
indifferent traffic spewing diesel —
they are everywhere exhausted.

Eternal spring, incongruous at these heights
in these emerald hills memory cradles
the disappeared — Inca kings and poets
legions of the faithful — their silent
skeletons slumber in the blood-soaked earth —

they are everywhere terraced in the mist
while splintered sunlight glimmers along
the leafy avenues and all the pretty painted
women stroll, twirling their colorful parasols.

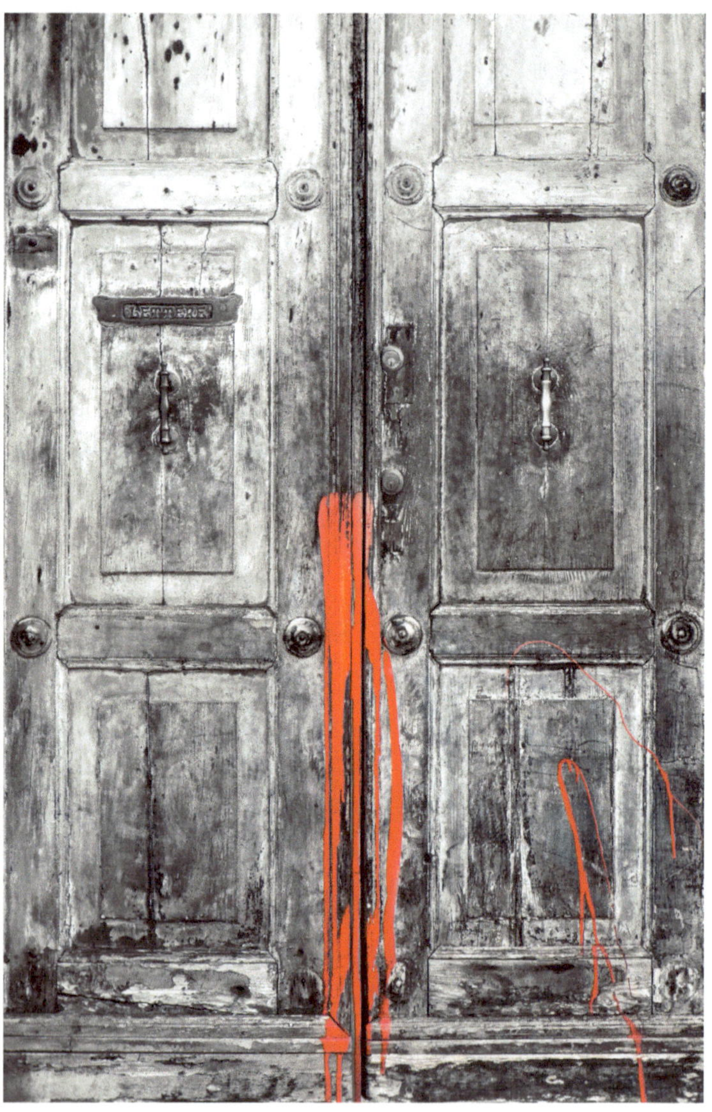

In the Holy Land

In the Holy Land
Another severed head rolls
Allahu Akbar!

In Jerusalem
Murder in the synagogue
Israeli tanks roll

Into Palestine
Innocent children buried
Their mothers wailing

The world's cross to bear
Father, son and other ghosts
Haunt the cold stone church

Where a candle burns
Ancient winds shiver the night
The candle flickers

Across the Sand the Pipers Run

Along the coast of Mexico
beyond the reach of winter snow
both travelers and pirates go
escaping strife. A different life

where on the shore the children play
as shadows spill across the bay.
Fifty pesos their mother's pay.
A life is spent to make the rent.

While at the bar cigars are smoked;
tequila shots for hedge fund blokes
and others who with egos stoked
sing songs of greed, as if they need

to celebrate their piracy
investment bankers' lunacy
corrupting moral currency.
And with their sin the tide rolls in.

The Masters of the Universe
spew out the lines that they've rehearsed
to justify their bulging purse.
Where's the onus? Grab that bonus!

And out at sea beyond the reef
in distant lands there's no relief
from money's grip and false belief.
And with their doubt the tide rolls out.

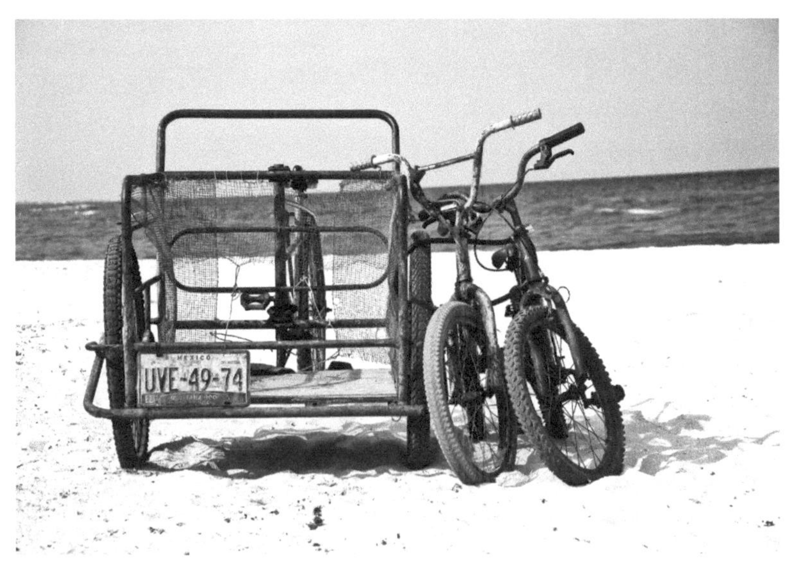

Underfoot the earthquake rumbles
Mayan temples start to crumble
one more round, the pirates stumble
back to their beds with aching heads.

Icy blood their hearts are pumping
the Wall Street whores, see them humping
Pensioners absorb the thumping
Their future lost. A brutal cost.

Across the sand the pipers run.
Two lovers dance beneath the sun
their laughter rings for everyone.
Another day, the palm trees sway.

Hutterite Strawberries

In northern Montana,
on the outskirts of Choteau,
I stopped by the roadside
intrigued by a sign:
Hutterite Strawberries
$2.00 a Basket.

A pair of young women,
in modest long dresses,
their straw colored hair
pinned up in bright scarves,
stood at a long table
in a cottonwood's shade
with their baskets of berries
arranged in strict rows.

Are you from around here?
The taller one probed,
then asked if in stopping
I'd stay for awhile
or move on like the rest
who are just passing through.

Dazed by her beauty
and brazen demeanor,
I stammered and stuttered
while watching a blush
leap out of her bodice,
race up her long neck,
then careen through her cheeks
to the lobes of her otherwise
unadorned ears.

She offered a taste
with a look that enchanted,
so I took her ripe berry
and bit into its swell.

That Hutterite Helen
looked on with delight
as the summer erupted
inside my parched mouth
and unleashed on my tongue
a juice so seductive
I was tempted to linger
for an hour or two
to share in the sweetness
of her ripe summer fruit
as I might once have done
before one reckless thing
led to another.

Yes, I might have discovered
her God of salvation
in a sweet-sticky-frantic
summer entangle,
but opted for safety,
alone heading home
on a two lane meander
with those Hutterite strawberries
perched on my lap
and my timeworn brown fingers
stained red by their juice.

Where Barns Once Stood

Behind locked gates where barns once stood,
within their halls of stone and glass,
the captains in their castles pass

their easy days and festive nights
among their comrades from the east
who made their bank and now they feast

on western land and grass-fed beef.
They frolic under mountain skies
and pay young guides to cast their flies

on pristine waters I once fished
in youthful freedom's precious light.
They've bought it all, it's locked up tight,

secured by wire and a lease.
Likewise these fields where I grew hale
building fence and bucking bales.

The landscape's changed, the solitude
has been exchanged for merriment
made possible by money spent

on marketing our quiet town
as one more stop along the route
of minstrels who, with golden flutes,

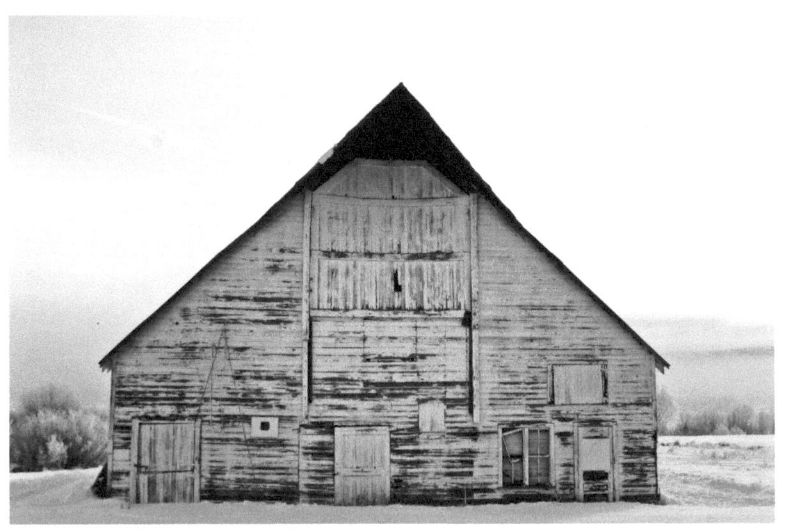

bring revelers our way. Oh look!
Another festival draws near.
A caravan of light appears

and in the streets the crowd awaits
the players with their retinue;
the media; the revenue!

But never mind all that my love.
Out here beyond the crowds and sleaze
There's river music on the breeze.

No one will see us in this barn.
Let's celebrate this night and dance.
Tonight might be our final chance.

Flowers

Jack, father of the bridegroom, button down East
Coast, holding court in pressed khakis, his navy blue
Blazer sporting brass buttons, drains another scotch

And on the peaty exhalation explains how
He shorted the market in two thousand eight
And used some of the profits to purchase this ranch.

He doesn't ride horses but he wears his hat well
So I'm happy to stand with him here at the bar
Drinking toasts to Nathaniel, his son and my friend

And to Daisy, the bride, *the flower from Berkeley*,
Jack says with a smile, though he privately wishes
She'd been plucked from the gardens of Wellesley
    or Smith.

Still, Daisy's a charmer, a vibrant addition
To the family bouquet of débutante women.

Lily, mother of the bride, draped in gossamer
Her braided silver hair and bangled wrists glinting
In the Montana sun, takes another toke and

On the pungent exhalation tells me something
About the Feng Shui of this place isn't quite right—
She doesn't feel centered. Still, I've been watching her

Glide through these festivities, trailing patchouli
As if on a cloud, captivating all with an
Insouciant air reminiscent of the women

I knew and loved and left in college—and even
After college. Ephemeral flowers, they bloomed
For a time, each in their short season, then floated

Away on the breeze. The way Lily is floating.

Some Observations from the Steaming Bean Café Late One Afternoon

A moment ago
with the afternoon fading
a tourist arrived

dressed like a cowboy
in stiff jeans and a Stetson.
He wants to fit in.

From under his hat
he orders a soy latte
with an extra shot

then proceeds to sit
at the table next to mine.
I notice his boots

which have been polished
to a slick-smooth urban sheen.
They've never kicked shit

or skimmed the dance floor
with a Wyoming cowgirl
who's looking for love

under the moonlight
in the back of a pick up
on Saturday night.

Next to the window
at a table strewn with books
three girls are giggling.

They look to be friends
but I sense they are rivals.
The hunt has begun.

Seems there's a new guy
who's checked into chemistry.
They say he is hot.

Some things never change.
Despite the new uniforms
the game is still played.

Save for the hardware
shot through lobes and brows and tongues
and all their tattoos

these girls are the same
as those I knew in high school
in the 70s.

Well, not exactly.
They communicate with thumbs
on cellular phones

drink gilded coffees
like the sweet macchiatos
they're sipping through straws

while studying French
and plotting their strategies
for trumping their friends.

I'm thinking I'll write
some kind of poem today
about all I've seen

in such a short span
while I sat drinking coffee
in the Steaming Bean.

I grab my notebook
and begin scribbling notes
on a blank white page.

The high school girls leave.
The tourist has paid his bill.
The café is still.

In shadows I glimpse
images arrayed in strange
juxtaposition:

My old worn out boots.
My daughter in Wyoming.
And her boyfriend's truck.

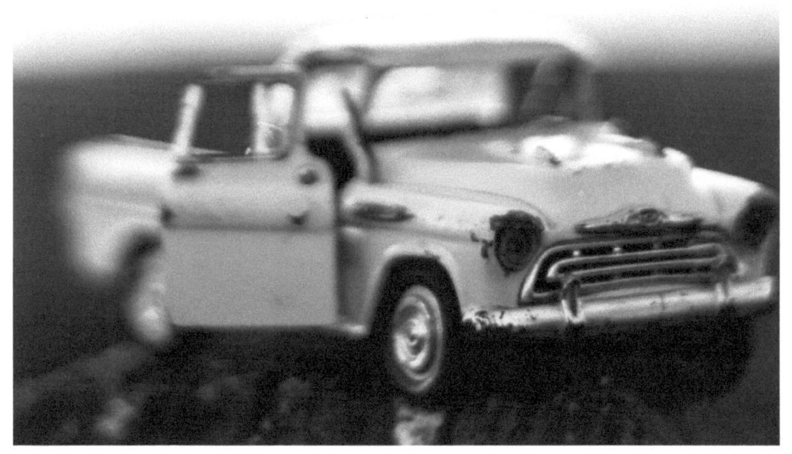

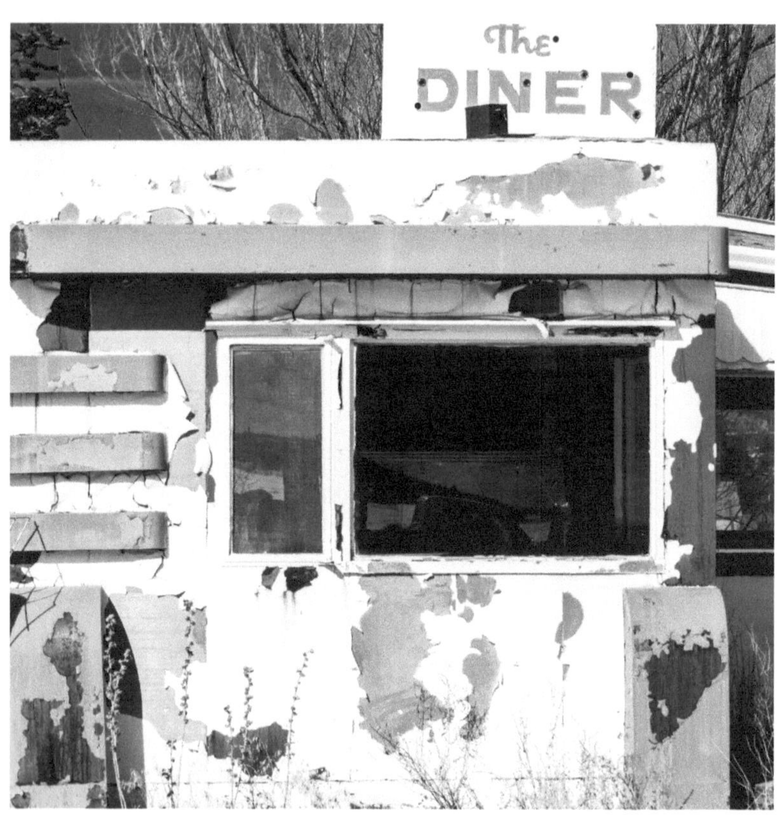
The
DINER

Hunger

It's too late in the day
to begin another poem

or dismember myself,
which is really the same thing.

And besides,
I'm hungry.

About the Author

Writer and businessman; educator and adventurer; father and humanitarian ... Lawrence Gregory is married to photographer Birgit Gutsche. They currently live in the rarefied air and revelatory light of northern New Mexico.

www.ingramcontent.com/pod-product-compliance
Lightning Source LLC
LaVergne TN
LVHW052308100826
845147LV00006B/703